TASHLULTUM LEVY

Introduction to Nocturnal Judasim

Ancient Judaism

Contents

I

Introduction

1

Introduction to "Nocturnal Judaism

In the vibrant tapestry of religious and cultural expressions that shape our world, Nocturnal Judaism emerges as a unique and compelling path, especially for those in the African-American community seeking a sense of wholeness, and purpose. This book, "Nocturnal Judaism" is not just an exploration of faith; it is an invitation to a journey that intertwines deep historical roots with the quest for personal and communal identity.

At its core, Nocturnal Judaism is more than a religion; it is a convergence of history, culture, spirituality, and identity. It reaches back into the rich soils of our past, drawing from the ancient wisdom of Jewish traditions and the profound spiritual heritage of Africa, creating a narrative that resonates deeply with the African-American experience. This faith acknowledges the struggles, celebrates the resilience, and embraces the diverse tapestry of stories that define the black community in America.

For those who may be skeptical about the role of religion, particularly in an age where secularism and skepticism are on the rise, Nocturnal Judaism offers a different perspective. It's not just about belief in a higher power, although that is a significant aspect for many; it's about finding a sense of wholeness, understanding one's history, and embracing a purpose that transcends the individual. It's about connecting with a community that shares a collective memory and a common hope for the future.

Nocturnal Judaism speaks to those who yearn for a deeper understanding of their cultural identity and heritage. It offers a spiritual framework that is inextricably linked with the rhythms of nature, the lunar cycles, and the transformative power of the night. This connection provides a unique space for reflection, growth, and connection, which is often missing in the hustle of our daily lives.

This faith also addresses the pressing need for social justice, community support, and ethical living, reflecting the values and aspirations of the African-American community. It provides a platform for dialogue, activism, and community building, aligning spiritual practice with the fight for equality and dignity for all.

As you turn these pages, you will discover the rich spiritual and cultural expressions of Nocturnal Judaism, from its music and art to its unique interpretations of sacred texts. You will explore its daily rhythms, its celebrations, and its deep commitment to community and personal growth. This book is an invitation to all, regardless of your beliefs or background, to explore a path that offers healing, understanding, and a profound sense of belonging.

Nocturnal Judaism is not just a faith; it's a journey back to oneself, a journey to wholeness, and a journey towards a future where every individual can find their place and purpose. Whether you believe in God or seek a connection with your heritage and community, this book and the path it outlines offer a gateway to something profound and transformative. Welcome to "Nocturnal Judaism"

2

Overview of Nocturnal Judaism

Nocturnal Judaism, a vibrant and distinct form of Jewish religious expression, has evolved uniquely among its practitioners, particularly within the African American community. It emphasizes the symbolic and spiritual significance of nighttime and lunar cycles, intertwining these elements deeply into its rituals, teachings, and cultural practices. Unlike mainstream Judaism, which largely follows a solar calendar, Nocturnal Judaism places greater emphasis on the lunar calendar, reflecting a profound connection to the rhythms of the natural world.

This form of Judaism also integrates aspects of Black history and culture, creating a rich tapestry that honors both Jewish heritage and African American identity. It's a living tradition that adapts ancient Jewish wisdom to contemporary contexts, addressing the unique spiritual, cultural, and social needs of its followers.

3

Purpose and Scope of the Book

This book, "Introduction to Nocturnal Judaism," is crafted with the intent to unveil the rich layers of this unique tradition. Aimed at both the uninitiated and those familiar with Jewish practices, this work seeks to provide a thorough understanding of Nocturnal Judaism's history, beliefs, and customs. It explores how this faith has shaped and been shaped by the experiences of African American Jews, highlighting its significance in the broader context of Jewish diversity.

The scope of this book extends from the historical roots of Nocturnal Judaism to its modern-day practices and cultural expressions. It covers fundamental beliefs, sacred texts, rituals, and the community's role, also delving into the challenges and opportunities faced by practitioners in contemporary society.

4

Methodology and Sources Used

The research and compilation of this book are grounded in a combination of scholarly research, religious texts, and first-hand accounts from practitioners of Nocturnal Judaism. Historical analyses provide context and trace the evolution of the faith, while contemporary sources offer insight into its current practices and place in modern society.

Primary sources, including key texts of Nocturnal Judaism and interviews with community leaders, form the backbone of this work. Secondary sources, such as scholarly articles and books on Jewish history and African American religious practices, offer additional perspectives and help situate Nocturnal Judaism within a broader religious and cultural framework.

Throughout, this book maintains a respectful and sensitive approach, acknowledging the diversity within Jewish practices and the unique intersection of Jewish and African American identities. It aims to be an informative and enlightening journey for those who wish to understand and appreciate the depth and breadth of Nocturnal Judaism.

II

Historical Background

5

Origins of Nocturnal Judaism

The inception of Nocturnal Judaism is a tale woven from the threads of history, spirituality, and cultural identity. Its roots can be traced back to the ancient practices of Judaism, yet it stands distinct, having evolved through a unique synthesis of Jewish traditions and African diasporic experiences. This evolution reflects a journey of resilience, adaptation, and profound spiritual introspection.

Nocturnal Judaism emerged as a response to the historical circumstances faced by Africans diaspora communities, particularly those in the Americas. Enslaved Africans brought to the New World were often forced to abandon their indigenous spiritual practices. However, they found resonances of their spiritual heritage within the folds of Judaism, a religion that was also practiced by some of their oppressors and fellow slaves.

The lunar cycle, central to traditional Jewish observance, found a new expression in Nocturnal Judaism. For these communities, the night became a time of spiritual reflection, community gathering, and a symbol of hope amidst the darkness of their circumstances. The moon's phases, reflecting the cycles of struggle and renewal, became deeply emblematic of their own experiences.

6

Evolution and Key Milestones

The evolution of Nocturnal Judaism is marked by several key milestones. Initially, its practices were clandestine, intertwined with the oral traditions and covert gatherings of enslaved peoples. Over time, as African Americans began to forge their distinct cultural and religious identities, Nocturnal Judaism was established as a form of Judaism that took on a more structured form.

A significant milestone in the development of Nocturnal Judaism was the establishment of the first black Nocturnal synagogue in America. These institutions are becoming a center for cultural preservation, theological exploration, and the fusion of Jewish and African American cultural practices.

Another pivotal moment was the formal recognition of Nocturnal Judaism as a distinct spiritual path within the broader Jewish community. This recognition was not just a religious milestone but also a social and cultural acknowledgment of the unique journey of African American Jews.

The civil rights movement in the United States further shaped the idea of Nocturnal Judaism. Where Jewish teachings on justice and liberation found a powerful echo in the struggle for civil rights, leading to an enriched understanding of Jewish theology through the lens of African American experiences of oppression and resistance.

7

Intersection with Black History and Identity

The intersection of Nocturnal Judaism with Black history and identity is profound. It represents a journey of double consciousness – being both Jewish and African American, and navigating the complexities of these intertwined identities.

Nocturnal Judaism offers a spiritual framework that acknowledges and celebrates the African heritage within Jewish practice. It reinterprets Jewish rituals, holidays, and scriptures in ways that resonate with the African American experience. For instance, the story of Exodus in the Hebrew Bible takes on a powerful metaphorical meaning, symbolizing the journey from slavery to freedom.

Moreover, Nocturnal Judaism contributes to the broader discourse on race, identity, and religion. It challenges conventional narratives and offers a unique perspective on the diversity within the Jewish community.

In , Nocturnal Judaism stands as a testament to the resilience and adaptive capacity of faith. It is a living tradition that continues to evolve, echoing the ongoing journey of African American Jews as they navigate their dual heritage and contribute to the rich tapestry of global Judaism.

III

Core Beliefs and Principles

8

Basic Tenets of Nocturnal Judaism

Nocturnal Judaism, while rooted in the broader Judaic tradition, has developed its distinct set of beliefs and principles. At its core, it embraces the fundamental tenets of Judaism, such as belief in one God, the importance of community, and the pursuit of justice and righteousness. However, it interprets these tenets through a lens that deeply intertwines the African American experience with Jewish spirituality.

A central belief in Nocturnal Judaism is the idea of liberation and redemption, not just as historical or future events, but as ongoing processes that individuals and communities actively participate in. This belief is heavily influenced by the history of slavery and the continuous struggle for equality and justice in the African American community.

Another key tenet is the emphasis on communal worship and solidarity. Nocturnal Judaism places a strong focus on community gatherings, often during the evening or night, as times for communal prayer, reflection, and support. This practice fosters a sense of belonging and strength in unity, crucial for communities that have historically faced marginalization.

9

Unique Aspects Differentiating It from Traditional Judaism

Nocturnal Judaism differentiates itself from traditional Judaism in several ways. One of the most notable distinctions is its emphasis on the lunar calendar and the symbolic significance of the moon. While traditional Judaism also follows a lunar calendar, Nocturnal Judaism imbues the lunar phases with additional spiritual meanings that resonate with the African American experience.

The interpretation of religious texts in Nocturnal Judaism often reflects the dual heritage of its adherents. Biblical stories and Jewish teachings are reexamined and retold in ways that highlight themes of resilience, struggle, and liberation, mirroring the historical and contemporary experiences of African Americans.

Moreover, Nocturnal Judaism incorporates elements of African spiritual traditions, music, and storytelling into its practices. This syncretism creates a rich tapestry of worship and community life that is distinct from more conventional Jewish practices.

10

The Role of Lunar Wisdom and Nighttime Practices

In Nocturnal Judaism, the moon is more than just a celestial body marking time; it is a source of wisdom and a symbol of the community's endurance and adaptability. The phases of the moon are seen as reflective of life's cyclical nature - from darkness to light, from hardship to liberation.

Nighttime practices in Nocturnal Judaism are not merely due to the practicalities of the lunar calendar but are imbued with deep spiritual significance. Night, traditionally a time of danger and fear, transforms into a sacred time for reflection, learning, and community bonding. These gatherings often feature storytelling, singing, and dancing, blending Jewish rituals with African American cultural expressions.

These practices serve several purposes. They reinforce communal bonds, provide spiritual nourishment, and offer a space for collective healing. Nighttime becomes a time when the community can come together, away from the gaze and pressures of the outside world, to connect with their heritage and with each other.

In , the core beliefs and principles of Nocturnal Judaism create a unique spiritual path that honors its dual heritage. Through its distinctive practices and interpretations, it provides a meaningful framework for its followers to explore their identity, faith, and the world around them.

11

Discovering and Fulfilling Purpose

A fundamental principle in Nocturnal Judaism is the encouragement and facilitation for individuals to discover and fulfill their unique purpose. This belief is deeply rooted in the understanding that every person is born with a distinct role to play in the fabric of the community and the universe. The journey to discovering one's purpose is considered sacred, involving deep introspection, community guidance, and spiritual practices that align with the laws of vibration and the rhythms of the universe.

This tenet emphasizes the importance of personal growth and self-realization within the framework of Jewish and African American cultural heritage. It advocates for a proactive approach to spiritual and personal development, where individuals are encouraged to seek knowledge, engage in reflective practices, and participate in communal activities that foster self-awareness and purpose.

In essence, this addendum to the basic tenets of Nocturnal Judaism underscores the importance of self-discovery, alignment with universal vibrations, and community self-reliance. These principles serve as a guide for the community to navigate their unique path within the broader tapestry of Judaism and their African American heritage.

12

Working with the Spiritual Laws of Vibration

Nocturnal Judaism places significant emphasis on understanding and working with the spiritual laws of vibration that govern the universe. This concept draws upon the idea that everything in the universe, including human beings, is in a constant state of vibration. The different frequencies and patterns of these vibrations influence our physical, emotional, and spiritual well-being.

The community engages in practices such as playing music, meditation, prayer, listening to music like Jazz and Chromatic Jazz, and dance, which are believed to harmonize individual vibrations with the universal flow. These practices are not only seen as ways to connect with the divine but also as tools for personal transformation and alignment with one's purpose.

Understanding and aligning with these vibrations is considered crucial for personal growth and the fulfillment of one's destiny. It is believed that by attuning to the right frequencies, individuals can manifest healing.

13

Reducing Reliance on Other Communities for Growth

A key principle in Nocturnal Judaism is the reduction of reliance on other communities to promote growth and self-sufficiency. This belief stems from a historical context where the African American community has often had to navigate systems that were not designed for their benefit. As such, Nocturnal Judaism advocates for a model of community development that is internally driven and self-sustaining.

This principle encourages the cultivation of resources within the community, whether they be educational, economic, or spiritual. It promotes the idea of self-reliance and the development of structures and systems that can support the community's unique needs and aspirations.

Furthermore, this approach fosters a sense of empowerment and resilience within the community. It is about building capacities that ensure not only the survival but the thriving of Nocturnal Judaism and its adherents, rooted in their rich heritage and guided by their spiritual beliefs.

IV

Addendum to Basic Tenets of Nocturnal Judaism

14

Self-Sufficiency in Manufacturing and Distribution

A crucial aspect of the principles of Nocturnal Judaism is the emphasis on becoming major manufacturers and distributors within the community. This shift is seen as vital in transitioning from the historically imposed role of consumers to that of producers and creators. The Black Jewish Community recognizes the need to develop and control its own production and distribution networks to reduce dependence on external systems that may not align with their needs or values.

This principle is rooted in a desire to assert economic independence and empowerment. By establishing their own manufacturing and distribution channels, the community can ensure that they are not only consumers but also key players in the economic process. This approach is about building resilience and sustainability within the community, allowing for greater control over the quality and availability of products and services that are essential to their way of life.

Developing Internal Networks to Support Community Members

The development of internal networks is a strategic priority for the Black Jewish Community. These networks aim to cut costs for community members, improve the quality of life, and foster a supportive economic ecosystem. The focus is on creating a framework where resources, knowledge, and opportunities circulate within the community, reinforcing the principles of mutual support and collective growth.

These networks are not limited to economic exchanges but extend to social and educational aspects, ensuring that all facets of community life are nurtured and strengthened. By pooling resources and expertise, the community can create a robust support system that is responsive to their specific needs and aspirations.

16

Cultivating Opportunities: Kosher Food Production and Employment

An essential component of these efforts is the cultivation of opportunities in areas such as kosher food production and job creation. Growing kosher foods not only meets the dietary requirements of the community but also ensures that these foods are produced in ways that align with their spiritual and ethical values. This initiative serves a dual purpose: it provides the community with high-quality, spiritually aligned food options and opens avenues for economic development and self-reliance.

Furthermore, the principle extends to creating job opportunities that are specifically designed to be filled by community members. This approach is about more than just employment; it's about building a workforce that is rooted in the community's cultural and spiritual values. By prioritizing the employment of community members, Nocturnal Judaism not only addresses economic needs but also reinforces a sense of communal identity and solidarity.

In summary, the addendum to the basic tenets of Nocturnal Judaism underscores the significance of self-sufficiency in manufacturing and distribution, the development of internal networks, and the cultivation of opportunities such as kosher food production and community-centric employment. These principles are fundamental in fostering an environment where the Black Jewish Community is not just surviving but thriving, anchored in their rich heritage and guided by a vision of economic empowerment and independence.

V

Sacred Texts and Literature

17

Sacred Texts and Literature

Nocturnal Judaism, like its traditional counterpart, places significant importance on sacred texts. However, it also incorporates writings that reflect its unique intersection of Jewish and African American heritage. Three pivotal texts in this regard are the bible, the Cuneiform writings of the Akkadian Empire, and the Tashlultum Mishna.

The Cuneiform texts of the Akkadian Empire are among the earliest known writings in human history. These texts provide invaluable insights into ancient Mesopotamian society, culture, and religion. For Nocturnal Judaism, these writings are more than historical artifacts; they are viewed as a source of ancient wisdom and a link to a past that predates even the Hebrew Bible.

The Tashlultum Mishna is a more recent but equally significant text in Nocturnal Judaism. Named after Tashlultum, a prominent figure in Akkadian history, this collection of writings offers interpretations of Jewish law and philosophy through the lens of the African American experience. The Tashlultum Mishna blends traditional Jewish teachings with insights from African spiritual traditions, providing a unique perspective on spiritual and ethical issues.

18

Interpretation and Study Methods

The study and interpretation of these sacred texts in Nocturnal Judaism are undertaken with a combination of traditional Jewish methods and approaches that draw on both ancient Akkadian information and African American cultural practices. This includes the use of PaRDeS, an acronym for Peshat (simple), Remez (hint), Derash (search), and Sod (secret), which represents the different levels of textual interpretation in Jewish tradition.

Additionally, interpretive methods involve communal study sessions that are often conducted at night, in keeping with the nocturnal aspect of the faith. These sessions encourage open discussion, debate, and the sharing of personal experiences, allowing the texts to be understood and applied in ways that resonate with the lives of the participants.

Music, storytelling, and oral tradition, integral to African American culture, also play a role in the interpretation of these texts. This approach adds a dynamic and experiential dimension to the study, making the ancient teachings more accessible and relevant to contemporary life.

19

Never Forget Your History

We have made significant contributions to the development of knowledge and interpretation of Nocturnal Judaism's sacred texts. Our work is instrumental in uncovering and preserving the African roots present in these texts, as well as in highlighting the shared experiences of struggle, liberation, and resilience between Jewish and African American histories.

These contributions are not limited to academic research but extend to the practical application of these teachings in addressing social and ethical issues faced by the community. Our goal is to be at the forefront of social justice movements, drawing upon the wisdom of these texts to advocate for change and equality.

Our work has also involved the creation of new commentaries and writings that expand the understanding of traditional Jewish texts. These modern interpretations often focus on themes of empowerment, community building, and social responsibility, reflecting the unique perspective and needs of the Nocturnal Jewish community.

In , this chapter highlights the rich tapestry of sacred texts and literature that form the foundation of Nocturnal Judaism. The unique blend of ancient Cuneiform writings, the Tashlultum Mishna, and historical information from

Black scholars and leaders illustrate the diverse and dynamic nature of this faith tradition. Through its distinctive approach to interpretation and study, Nocturnal Judaism fosters a deep and meaningful engagement with its sacred texts, enriching the spiritual life of its adherents.

20

Ancient Numerology in Scriptural Interpretation

In Nocturnal Judaism, the study of sacred texts, particularly the Torah, is enhanced by an ancient method of interpretation that incorporates numerology and cosmic patterns. This unique approach reveals deeper meanings within the scriptural narratives, particularly evident in the interpretation of the seven days of creation.

1. First Day of Life in the Womb- The Mental Realm:
   - The act of creation itself symbolizes the initiation, represented by the number one, which in this context embodies the mental realm.
   - The creation of the heavens signifies the mind or the mental realm, while the earth represents the body or physical realm, reflecting the duality and balance inherent in the universe.

2. Second Day — The Physical Realm:
   - The number two, symbolizing duality and reflection, corresponds to the development of the physical realm.
   - The depiction of the earth as formless and the focus on the Spirit of God moving upon the waters alludes to the nascent stage of physical creation, where potentiality awaits manifestation.

3. Third Day – The Soul Realm:

  - This day is marked by the creation of light and its separation from darkness, a metaphor for the soul realm.

  - The differentiation of light and dark symbolizes the soul's journey from ignorance to enlightenment, embodying spiritual awakening and discernment.

4. Fourth Day – Realm of Gifts:

  - The evaluation of light as 'good' and its separation from darkness signifies the realm of gifts, where inherent talents and virtues are recognized and cultivated.

5. Fifth Day – Realm of Purpose:

  - The naming of day and night and the establishment of time markers such as hours and months indicate the emergence of purpose.

  - This day suggests a cosmic order, akin to the solar and lunar calendars and their role in the formation of the 12 tribes, each with a distinct vibration and purpose.

This numerological interpretation of the creation narrative in the Torah offers a profound understanding of the universal patterns and principles. It aligns with the belief that the Torah uses numbers not just as quantitative values but as symbols teaching patterns within the universe. This approach is reminiscent of the seven white keys on a piano or the first seven letters of the Akkadian cuneiform alphabet, each holding a unique sound and meaning.

The Beginning of LIFE: A Numerological Perspective

The opening verses of Genesis, describing the creation of the heavens and the earth, are seen through this numerological lens as an allegorical representation of the universe's foundational principles. The formlessness and void of the earth, the darkness over the deep, and the divine spirit hovering over the waters are interpreted as symbolic elements representing the mental, physical, and soul realms in the cosmic order.

This interpretation, unique to Nocturnal Judaism, blends traditional Jewish teachings with broader esoteric concepts, offering a rich and multi-layered understanding of the Torah's narratives. It's important to recognize that these interpretations are specific to Nocturnal Judaism and may vary from other Jewish interpretive traditions. This approach reflects the community's endeavor to find deeper meaning and relevance in ancient texts, aligning them with their spiritual and cultural identity.

Sound Healing and the Torah - The Language of Sozo Keys

In Nocturnal Judaism, sound healing is a revered and intricate practice that draws upon the ancient wisdom of the Torah and the spiritual language of sounds, known as Sozo keys. This chapter delves into the profound relationship between sound, healing, and spiritual growth, offering insights into how the Torah portions guide the identification and use of specific sounds for healing purposes.

Understanding Sozo Keys

Sozo keys represent a unique concept within Nocturnal Judaism, where every sound is believed to carry a specific vibrational energy, akin to a language. This concept parallels the idea that each element in the periodic table has its distinct properties. Similarly, every note on the piano is not just a musical tone but embodies a specific language, carrying unique vibrational qualities that can unlock deeper aspects of the self.

Using Torah Portions to Identify Healing Sounds

The Torah, in its rich tapestry of narratives, laws, and teachings, is seen as a source of divine wisdom that also encodes specific vibrational energies in its text. In Nocturnal Judaism, each Torah portion is associated with particular sounds or Sozo keys. These sounds are identified through a combination of traditional scriptural study and intuitive understanding of the vibrational qualities inherent in the Torah's words.

Practitioners of sound healing in Nocturnal Judaism study the Torah portions to discern the specific Sozo keys that resonate with the themes, teachings, or spiritual energies of these passages. This practice is not just about understanding the textual meaning but also about experiencing the Torah as a living, vibrational entity that communicates through sound.

Sound Healing for Mind and Soul

In Nocturnal Judaism, sound healing is employed to address various aspects of mental and spiritual well-being. The identified Sozo keys from the Torah portions are used in meditative practices, communal worship, and personal reflection to facilitate healing. These sounds are believed to resonate with the inner self, helping to address psychological triggers and emotional blockages.

The practice of sound healing involves more than just listening to tones; it is an immersive experience where the individual engages with the vibrational energies of the sounds. This engagement can lead to a profound healing process, where the mind and soul are harmonized, and a deeper sense of peace and spiritual connectedness is achieved.

From Meaningless Notes to a Language of Healing

In this approach, the notes of music are transformed from mere sounds into a language of healing. Each note, corresponding to a Sozo key, carries a specific meaning and purpose. When played or sung, these notes interact with the listener's vibrational energy, facilitating a process of inner transformation and healing.

This chapter emphasizes that sound healing in Nocturnal Judaism is a holistic practice that goes beyond physical healing. It is about aligning the individual with the deeper vibrations of the universe, as encoded in the Torah, and unlocking the potential for profound spiritual growth and self-realization.

In , the practice of sound healing through the Torah and the concept of Sozo keys in Nocturnal Judaism represents a unique synthesis of ancient scriptural wisdom and the transformative power of sound. It offers a pathway to healing that is deeply spiritual, connecting individuals with the deeper vibrations of their inner selves and the universe.

22

Ancient Exegesis and Sound Healing - Bridging Akkadian and Hebrew Wisdom

Recreating Ancient Cuneiform Texts: A Path to Understanding

In Nocturnal Judaism, there is a profound interest in recreating and under-standing ancient texts, particularly those in Cuneiform from the Akkadian Empire. This process involves converting Hebrew texts into Cuneiform script, enabling a deeper exploration of ancient wisdom. By delving into the Akkadian language and its commentaries, practitioners gain a unique perspective on biblical narratives and laws, drawing parallels between Akkadian and Hebrew exegesis.

The Authority and Content of Akkadian and Hebrew Exegesis

The authority of texts in both Mesopotamian and Hebrew traditions is grounded in their perceived divine origin. In Mesopotamia, this included cultic, liturgical, and divinatory texts, while in the Hebrew tradition, it primarily encompassed the Torah and the writings of the prophets. The scholarly interpretation of these texts, whether in Akkadian commentaries or rabbinic Midrash, derives its authority from this divine connection, perceived as a continuous transmission of knowledge from ancient sages or prophets.

The content of these commentaries, though varying in focus, reflects a similar conceptual framework. Mesopotamian texts predominantly dealt with omens and technical literature, while Hebrew commentaries often focused on law, narrative, and prophecy. Despite these differences, both traditions viewed their respective texts as divine laws or pronouncements, linking them conceptually.

Hermeneutics: The Art of Interpretation

In both traditions, the primary goal of exegesis is to clarify and deepen the understanding of sacred texts. This is often achieved through glossing, paraphrasing, and sometimes more complex methods like harmonization and specification. For instance, Akkadian commentaries might resolve contradictions in omens by contextualizing or reinterpreting them, a technique mirrored in the harmonization efforts of rabbinic Midrash.

Sound Healing through Sozo Keys: Unlocking the Inner Self

Building on this ancient wisdom, Nocturnal Judaism employs the concept of Sozo keys in its practice of sound healing. These keys, represented by specific notes or tones, are believed to unlock aspects of the inner self, facilitating healing of the mind and addressing psychological triggers. Each note in this system is imbued with meaning, turning what were once seen as 'meaningless notes' into a profound language of healing.

Through the study of Torah portions and their corresponding Sozo keys, practitioners of Nocturnal Judaism engage in a form of sound healing that is deeply connected to their spiritual and cultural heritage. This approach recognizes each note's unique vibrational quality, akin to the elements in the periodic table, and uses these vibrations to align the individual with the universe's natural rhythms.

In Nocturnal Judaism, the ancient art of exegesis and the modern practice of sound healing converge, creating a rich tapestry of spiritual exploration. By studying and reinterpreting ancient texts, both from the Hebrew and Akkadian traditions, and employing the transformative power of sound through Sozo keys, practitioners find a unique path to spiritual growth, healing, and a deeper understanding of the universe.

Ancient Cuneiform Texts and Hebrew Exegesis - The Interplay of Sound and Symbol

Recreating Ancient Cuneiform and Its Influence on Hebrew Exegesis

In Nocturnal Judaism, a profound connection is drawn between the ancient Cuneiform texts of the Akkadian Empire and Hebrew scriptural interpretation. The process of recreating and speaking ancient Cuneiform texts is seen not just as an academic exercise, but as a spiritual practice that brings deeper insights into the Torah and other sacred writings.

Akkadian Commentaries and Early Hebrew Exegesis

The study of Akkadian commentaries and their relationship with early Hebrew exegesis has revealed significant parallels in hermeneutics, content, and the construction of textual authority. As noted by scholars like W. G. Lambert, and detailed in the work of Uri Gabbay, the ancient Mesopotamian commentaries share various features with rabbinic Midrash and the Pesharim literature of the Qumran community.

1. Authority:
   - In both Mesopotamian and Hebrew traditions, texts with divine attribution hold the highest authority. This includes cultic and liturgical texts, prophecies, and narratives believed to be divinely inspired.
   - Commentaries, whether Akkadian or rabbinic, carry scholarly authority, regarded as interpretations derived from divine wisdom transmitted across generations.

2. Content:
   - Hebrew commentaries typically focus on law, narratives, and prophecies. In contrast, Akkadian commentaries often deal with omens, medical texts, and lexical studies, but they share a similar conceptual foundation in viewing these as divine laws or predictions.
   - Both traditions engage in harmonizing contradictions and specifying general statements, often resolving apparent conflicts by delineating specific situations or interpretations.

3. Hermeneutics:
   - The goal of both Akkadian and Hebrew exegesis is often to clarify the meaning of texts, whether by glossing, paraphrasing, or resolving contradictions.
   - This process aims at simplicity and clarity, ensuring that the sacred texts are accessible and relevant to contemporary practitioners.

Sound Healing through Torah and Cuneiform

In Nocturnal Judaism, the integration of ancient Cuneiform study with Hebrew scriptures has led to the development of a unique sound healing practice. This involves using the Torah portion to identify specific sounds or "Sozo keys," which are believed to unlock healing and spiritual awakening.

1. Sozo Keys: The Language of Sound
   - Each note or sound, akin to the elements of the periodic table, is seen as a

unique language with specific healing properties.

- By recreating sounds from Cuneiform texts and aligning them with the Torah readings, practitioners can tap into ancient vibrations that promote mental and spiritual healing.

2. Application in Worship and Meditation

- The Sozo keys are used in various aspects of worship and meditation, allowing participants to experience the Torah and ancient texts as living, vibrational entities.

- This practice goes beyond traditional reading and interpretation, inviting a deeper, more experiential engagement with the sacred texts.

In this chapter, we explored the intricate relationship between ancient Akkadian Cuneiform texts and Hebrew scriptural interpretation, particularly within the context of Nocturnal Judaism. The study and recreation of these ancient texts, coupled with the innovative practice of sound healing through Sozo keys, demonstrate a unique approach to spiritual growth and understanding. This synthesis of ancient wisdom and modern practice highlights the dynamic and evolving nature of Nocturnal Judaism, where ancient traditions are not only preserved but also imbued with new life and relevance.

24

Ancient Texts and Sound Healing - The Language of Sozo Keys

Integrating Ancient Cuneiform Texts with Hebrew Scriptures

Nocturnal Judaism, in its approach to sacred texts, uniquely incorporates the ancient cuneiform texts of the Akkadian Empire alongside traditional Hebrew Scriptures. This integration allows for a profound synthesis of ancient Near Eastern wisdom with Jewish spiritual heritage, enriching the community's understanding of their faith and history.

Cuneiform and Hebrew Exegesis: A Comparative Study

Drawing on the work of scholars like Uri Gabbay, this chapter explores the parallels and intersections between Akkadian commentaries and early Hebrew exegesis. As highlighted in Gabbay's research, both traditions share hermeneutical concerns, techniques, and tools, despite the differences in the nature of the corpora they address. This comparison deepens the understanding of scriptural interpretation in Nocturnal Judaism, revealing a shared foundation in the quest for meaning and clarity in ancient texts.

Authority in Textual Interpretation

Both Mesopotamian and rabbinic traditions distinguish between divine and scholarly authority in their texts. In Nocturnal Judaism, this concept is expanded to include the divine inspiration found in both the Hebrew Scriptures and the Akkadian texts. The study of these texts is approached with reverence, acknowledging their sacred origin and the continuous transmission of wisdom they represent.

Content and Hermeneutics: Bridging Ancient Traditions

While Hebrew commentaries traditionally focus on law, narrative, and prophecy, and Mesopotamian commentaries deal primarily with omens and technical literature, Nocturnal Judaism finds a common ground in their underlying religious and conceptual perceptions. Both traditions view their respective texts as divine pronouncements, offering guidance and insight into the divine will.

The hermeneutical process in Nocturnal Judaism, influenced by these ancient methods, seeks to uncover the deeper meanings within the texts. This involves harmonizing contradictions, specifying general statements, and interpreting omens and prophecies in a contemporary context, while maintaining the simplicity and clarity that are hallmarks of both traditions.

Sound Healing and Sozo Keys: Unlocking the Language of the Torah

Incorporating the concept of Sozo keys, this chapter delves into the use of sound healing as a method of spiritual and physical healing within Nocturnal Judaism. The Torah portions are studied not just for their textual content but also for their intrinsic sound patterns, believed to be encoded within the Hebrew language and the ancient Akkadian cuneiform.

Each note and sound is considered a language in itself, much like elements in the periodic table, carrying specific vibrational energies. These energies, when unlocked and utilized through chanting, singing, or instrumental music, offer healing for the mind and soul. They address psychological triggers and emotional blockages, transforming what were once perceived as meaningless notes into a profound language of healing.

This Chapter presents a unique perspective on the study and interpretation of sacred texts in Nocturnal Judaism. It highlights the integration of ancient Mesopotamian and Hebrew traditions, offering a rich tapestry of spiritual wisdom. The incorporation of sound healing through Sozo keys further exemplifies the community's commitment to exploring and utilizing ancient wisdom in contemporary spiritual practices. This approach not only honors the historical roots of Nocturnal Judaism but also provides practical tools for personal and communal growth and healing.

VI

Rituals and Practices

25

Rituals and Practices

Daily Practices Specific to Nocturnal Judaism

In Nocturnal Judaism, daily practices are designed to align followers with their unique spiritual path and heritage. These practices often take place at night, embracing the quiet and introspective energy that darkness brings.

1. Evening Study and Meditation: Members of the community engage in nightly study sessions, where they delve into sacred texts, including the Torah, cuneiform texts, and other writings significant to Nocturnal Judaism. These sessions are often accompanied by meditation, where individuals reflect on the teachings and seek personal and spiritual insights.

2. Nocturnal Prayers: Special prayers and chants are recited at night, believed to carry a different energy and resonance due to the stillness and tranquility of the night. These prayers focus on protection, guidance, and the seeking of wisdom from the divine.

3. Dream Interpretation: Given the importance of dreams in many African traditions and their mention in Jewish texts, Nocturnal Judaism places a strong emphasis on dream interpretation. Community members often share and interpret their dreams as a way of receiving divine messages and

understanding their subconscious mind.

Sabbath and Holiday Observances

1. Sabbath (Shabbat) Observance: While the Sabbath is observed from Friday evening to Saturday evening in all Jewish traditions, Nocturnal Judaism emphasizes the onset of Shabbat at dusk as a particularly sacred time. Special services and community gatherings are held to welcome the Sabbath bride, often including singing, dancing, and drumming, which are integral to African heritage.

2. Holiday Observances: Traditional Jewish holidays are observed with specific practices that reflect the community's unique identity. For example, during Passover, traditional foods are infused with African flavors, and the story of Exodus is related to the history of slavery and liberation. Other holidays, like Sigd, Sukkot and Shavuot, are celebrated with an emphasis on community gathering and reflection.

Rites of Passage and Community Celebrations

1. Naming Ceremonies: Drawing from both Jewish and African traditions, naming ceremonies in Nocturnal Judaism are significant events. They often include music, dance, and the recitation of prayers and blessings specific to the community's heritage. Names are chosen to reflect the child's spiritual path and the parents' hopes for their future.

2. Coming of Age Rituals: Similar to the Bar/Bat Mitzvah in traditional Judaism, Nocturnal Judaism has its unique coming-of-age rituals, which may include elements like community service, a period of learning and preparation, and a celebratory ceremony that incorporates African and Jewish traditions.

3. Marriage Ceremonies: Weddings in Nocturnal Judaism blend Jewish marital customs with African traditions, such as the jumping of the broom, which

symbolizes sweeping away the old and welcoming the new. The ceremonies are rich with music, dance, and vibrant cultural expressions, celebrating the union of two souls and two families.

4. Community Festivals: In addition to religious holidays, Nocturnal Judaism celebrates festivals that honor African heritage and history, such as Juneteenth. These celebrations are times of joy, remembrance, and community bonding, often featuring storytelling, traditional foods, and communal activities.

This chapter outlines the rich tapestry of rituals and practices in Nocturnal Judaism, which are deeply embedded in both Jewish and African traditions. These practices provide a framework for daily living, spiritual growth, and community cohesion, reflecting the unique identity and heritage of the Nocturnal Jewish community. Through these rituals and observances, followers connect with their past, present, and future, forging a spiritual path that is both ancient and continually evolving.

26

The Three Pilgrimages and Daily Purpose

The Three Pilgrimages: Sugarplum, Daydream, and Nightmare

In Nocturnal Judaism, the metaphorical journeys of Sugarplum, Daydream, and Nightmare are deeply intertwined with Jewish festivals, reflecting the cycle of life, death, and resurrection—a recurring theme in the Torah and in human existence.

1. Sugarplum - Festival of Life (Pesach/Passover):
   - Symbolizing joy, rebirth, and freedom, the pilgrimage of Sugarplum corresponds with Pesach (Passover). This festival celebrates the Israelites' liberation from slavery in Egypt, marking a journey from hardship (Nightmare) to freedom and new beginnings (Sugarplum).

2. Daydream - Festival of Aspiration (Shavuot):
   - Representing hope, revelation, and future planning, Daydream aligns with Shavuot. This festival commemorates the giving of the Torah at Mount Sinai, symbolizing the aspiration for divine wisdom and spiritual growth.

3. Nightmare - Festival of Contemplation (Yom Kippur):
   - Symbolizing introspection, atonement, and overcoming challenges, Nightmare is reflected in Yom Kippur, the Day of Atonement. This solemn day is a

time for repentance, self-reflection, and seeking forgiveness, mirroring the transformative journey of Nightmare.

The Cycle of Life, Death, and Resurrection

The concept of life, death, and resurrection is a profound pattern observed throughout the Torah and is emblematic of the human experience:

- Conception and Birth: The journey begins with conception, a symbol of potential life and new beginnings. Birth, while a passage into life, also represents a form of 'death' to the previous existence within the womb, leading to a new life in the outside world.

- Life and Growth: Post-birth, life is a continuous process of growth, learning, and adaptation. This stage resonates with the pilgrimage of Daydream, where aspirations are nurtured.

- Transition and Transformation: In the cycle of life, there are moments of introspection and transformation, akin to the spiritual journey of Nightmare. These are times of inner struggle, leading to personal growth and renewal.

- Celebration and Renewal: The cycle culminates in a return to joy and celebration, echoing the spirit of Sugarplum. It's a time of recognizing the journey's completion and preparing for the next cycle of growth.

In Nocturnal Judaism, the three pilgrimages, aligned with key Jewish festivals, provide a framework for understanding the spiritual journey of life. Each stage—Sugarplum, Daydream, and Nightmare—corresponds to a phase in the cycle of life, death, and resurrection, reflecting the deep spiritual themes present in the Torah. These pilgrimages guide the community through the rhythms of life, offering insights and practices to navigate each stage with wisdom and resilience.

27

Practice, Practice, Practice

Creating an education plan that focuses on Black Jewish identity and history, while emphasizing a broad spectrum of skills and knowledge areas, involves integrating core Jewish studies with a rich exploration of Black history, culture, and contributions in various fields. Here's an updated plan with these considerations:

Early Childhood (Ages 3-5)

Jewish and Black Heritage Studies
  - Introduction to Jewish and Black Festivals: Learning about both Jewish holidays and significant moments in Black history through stories and activities.
  - Basic Hebrew and African Languages: Introduction to Hebrew and a selection of African languages relevant to the Black Jewish community.
  - Biblical and African Folktales: Sharing stories from Jewish texts and African folklore.
  - Values and Ethics: Focus on shared values in both Jewish and African cultures, like community, resilience, and justice.

Foundational Skills
  - Basic literacy, numeracy, and introductory science concepts.

- Basic arts and crafts, focusing on Jewish and African themes.
- Physical education with an emphasis on traditional African dances and games.

Primary Education (Ages 6-12)

Jewish and Black Heritage Studies

- Advanced Hebrew and African Languages: Progress in language skills, including reading and writing.
- Jewish and Black History: Study of Jewish history alongside African and African American history.
- Jewish and African American Rituals and Customs: Understanding traditions from both cultures.
- African Tribal Studies: Introduction to the history and culture of various African tribes.

Core Academic Subjects

- Mathematics with a focus on practical applications like the abacus.
- Science with a focus on contributions by Black scientists.
- Language Arts including literature from Jewish and Black authors.
- Social Studies with a global perspective, focusing on Jewish and African American narratives.

Specialized Courses

- Entrepreneurship and Innovation: Learning about Black and Jewish entrepreneurs and inventors.
- Art: Exploring art through the lens of Jewish and Black artists.
- Gardening and Environmental Science: Practical gardening skills and understanding of environmental stewardship.

Secondary Education (Ages 13-18)

Advanced Jewish and Black

Chapter 28

Jewish Holidays and Solstice Events

Jewish Holidays
  - Rosh Hashanah: The Jewish New Year, focusing on reflection, renewal, and the creation of the world.
  - Yom Kippur: The Day of Atonement, a day of fasting, prayer, and repentance.
  - Sukkot: The Feast of Tabernacles, commemorating the Israelites' journey in the wilderness.
  - Hanukkah: The Festival of Lights, celebrating the rededication of the Second Temple in Jerusalem.
  - Purim: Celebrating the saving of the Jewish people from Haman, as recounted in the Book of Esther.
  - Passover (Pesach): Commemorating the Exodus from Egypt.
  - Shavuot: Celebrating the giving of the Torah at Mount Sinai.

Solstice Events
  - Winter Solstice (Singing Solstice): A time for communal singing, reflection, and celebration of light during the darkest time of the year.
  - Summer Solstice: Acknowledging the longest day of the year, perhaps with themes of gratitude and the abundance of nature.

Sigd Festival

- Sigd festival can serve as a bridge between Ethiopian Jewish traditions and the broader Jewish and African American experiences.

Lord of Time Festival

- While specific information on the "Lord of Time" a festival that celebrates history, heritage, and the passage of time. This festival include: Exploring themes of time, history, and legacy in both Jewish and African American contexts.

- Cultural Performances: Music, dance, and drama that reflect the rich heritage of the Black Jewish community.

- Community Discussions: Panels and discussions on the significance of time in cultural and religious practices.

Rites of Passage for Black Jewish Americans

- Tailoring traditional Jewish rites like Bar/Bat Mitzvah ceremonies to celebrate African American heritage and history.

- Workshops and classes on significant figures and events in both Jewish and African American history.

- Encouraging community service as a rite of passage, reflecting values of both cultures.

Educational Focus Areas

- Cultural Education: A deep dive into the traditions, histories, and contributions of both the Jewish and African American communities.

- Spiritual Practices: Incorporating prayer and meditation practices from both traditions.

- Community Involvement: Engaging with both the local Jewish community and the broader African American community through service and cultural events.

This education plan aims to provide a rich, diverse, and inclusive learning experience, acknowledging and celebrating the unique intersection of Black and Jewish identities. The inclusion of the "Lord of Time" festival, alongside traditional Jewish holidays and solstice events, adds a unique dimension to the curriculum, allowing for the exploration of universal themes such as time, heritage, and the cyclical nature of life.

VII

Spiritual and Ethical Teachings

29

Spiritual Perspectives Unique to Nocturnal Judaism

Nocturnal Judaism, while rooted in traditional Jewish teachings, offers unique spiritual perspectives that reflect the distinct historical and cultural experiences of its community.

1. Integration of African Spiritual Heritage: Nocturnal Judaism incorporates elements of African spiritual traditions, enriching its religious practices and beliefs. This integration acknowledges the ancestral heritage of the community, bringing a deeper, more holistic understanding of spirituality.

2. Emphasis on the Lunar Cycle: The lunar cycle plays a significant role in Nocturnal Judaism, not just as a timekeeping system but as a spiritual symbol. The phases of the moon are seen as reflective of life's cyclical nature and are used to understand personal and communal rhythms.

3. Night as a Time for Spiritual Connection: The quiet and introspection offered by the night are harnessed for spiritual connection and growth. Nighttime practices, including prayer and meditation, are central, providing a unique setting for spiritual experiences and revelations.

Ethical Guidelines and Social Justice

Nocturnal Judaism places a strong emphasis on ethics and social justice, drawing upon both Jewish teachings and the African American experience of striving for equality and dignity.

1. Pursuit of Justice and Righteousness: Influenced by the prophetic tradition within Judaism and the civil rights legacy, Nocturnal Judaism actively engages in social justice issues. It promotes actions and teachings that advocate for fairness, equity, and the protection of the vulnerable.

2. Community Support and Solidarity: There is a strong focus on communal support and solidarity, especially in the face of adversity. The community is encouraged to stand together, supporting each other's struggles and celebrating each other's successes.

3. Ethical Stewardship: Environmental stewardship and ethical living are key aspects of the community's ethical guidelines. This includes sustainable practices and respect for all of creation, drawing on the belief that the earth and all its inhabitants are sacred.

Community and Individual Responsibilities

In Nocturnal Judaism, there is a balance between community and individual responsibilities, emphasizing the importance of each in spiritual and ethical living.

1. Community Responsibilities: The community is seen as a collective where each member plays a vital role. Responsibilities include educating the young, caring for the elderly, and providing support to those in need. The community is also responsible for maintaining cultural and spiritual traditions.

2. Individual Responsibilities: Each individual is encouraged to embark on a

personal spiritual journey while contributing to the community. This includes personal development, ethical living, and active participation in communal activities. Individuals are also encouraged to explore and develop their unique talents and gifts for the betterment of the community.

Nocturnal Judaism delves into the spiritual and ethical teachings unique to the community. These teachings blend traditional Jewish wisdom with African spiritual heritage and the community's historical experiences. The chapter emphasizes the importance of community and individual responsibilities in creating a just, supportive, and spiritually enriched community life.

30

15-The Dream of Equality

BO: The fifteenth reading from the Torah is named Bo, which means "come." The title comes from the first words of the first verse of the reading, which say, "Then the LORD said to Moses, '[Come] to Pharaoh, for I have hardened his heart" (Exodus 10:1). The portion begins by concluding the narrative of the ten plagues, the tenth of which is the slaying of the firstborn. To avoid the plague, the Israelites are given the instructions for the Passover sacrifice and the laws of the Feast of Unleavened Bread. Pharaoh finally consents to let Israel go, and they leave Egypt.

Torah Portion Title: "The Dream of Equality"

This Torah portion, inspired by the profound impact of Dr. Martin Luther King Jr. on civil rights and social justice, is titled "The Dream of Equality." It aims to offer a comprehensive study on his life, teachings, and enduring legacy, encouraging reflection and discussion on the themes of equality, justice, and nonviolent resistance.

Black History Torah Reading: Dr. Martin Luther King Jr.'s Life Journey and Legacy

Haftarah: Select Writings and Speeches of Dr. King

Other: Major Civil Rights Movements and Events

Portion Summary:

Dr. Martin Luther King Jr.'s Life Journey and Legacy

This portion of the Torah focuses on Dr. King's life, tracing his journey from his early years in Atlanta to becoming a prominent leader in the Civil Rights Movement. It examines his role in key events, his philosophy of nonviolent protest, and his efforts to achieve racial equality and social justice. The portion emphasizes Dr. King's impact on American society and the ongoing relevance of his message.

Haftarah: Select Writings and Speeches of Dr. King

The Haftarah section includes excerpts from Dr. King's most influential writings and speeches, including the "I Have a Dream" speech, "Letter from Birmingham Jail," and his Nobel Peace Prize acceptance speech. These selections highlight his eloquent advocacy for civil rights, his moral vision, and his hope for a society free of discrimination and injustice.

Gospels: Major Civil Rights Movements and Events

The Gospels reading covers significant events and movements in the Civil Rights era, such as the Montgomery Bus Boycott, the March on Washington, and the Selma to Montgomery marches. It connects these historical moments with Dr. King's leadership and the broader struggle for civil rights, demonstrating the collective effort and resilience in the face of adversity.

Notable quotes by Dr. Martin Luther King Jr.:

1. "I have a dream that my four little children will one day live in a nation where they will not be judged by the color of their skin, but by the content of their character."

2. "Injustice anywhere is a threat to justice everywhere."

3. "Darkness cannot drive out darkness; only light can do that. Hate cannot drive out hate; only love can do that."

4. "Our lives begin to end the day we become silent about things that matter."

5. "The time is always right to do what is right."

Portion Outline:

1. Childhood and Education – An exploration of Dr. King's early life, family background, and educational journey, shaping his views on civil rights.
2. Rise as a Civil Rights Leader – Dr. King's emergence as a national figure during pivotal events like the Montgomery Bus Boycott and his role in founding the Southern Christian Leadership Conference (SCLC).
3. Landmark Speeches and Writings – Analysis of Dr. King's key speeches and writings, exploring his rhetoric, ideology, and call for nonviolent resistance.
4. Significant Campaigns and Marches – The study of major civil rights campaigns and marches, including their impact and Dr. King's involvement, highlighting the strategic and moral challenges faced during these movements.
5. Nobel Peace Prize and Global Influence – Recognition of Dr. King's contributions to the cause of peace and equality, including his receipt of the Nobel Peace Prize and how his ideas influenced civil rights movements worldwide.
6. Challenges and Controversies – Examination of the challenges, criticisms, and controversies Dr. King faced, both from within and outside the civil rights movement, and how he addressed them.
7. Assassination and Legacy – Reflection on the circumstances and impact of Dr. King's assassination in 1968, and the ongoing influence of his life and teachings on contemporary social justice movements.
8. Continuing the Dream – Discussion on how Dr. King's vision for equality

and justice continues to resonate today, encouraging ongoing efforts towards achieving his dream of a fair and just society.

75

This Torah portion, "The Dream of Equality," serves as an educational and reflective tool to understand and appreciate the life and legacy of Dr. Martin Luther King Jr. It provides a comprehensive overview of his impact on the civil rights movement and offers insights into his philosophy of nonviolent resistance and his enduring vision for a world of equality and justice.

31

15th week

Chapter 1: Early Years and Education

1. In the days of yore, in the city of Atlanta within the land of Georgia, a child was born unto the lineage of King, a family steeped in the faith of the Lord and the righteous struggle for justice. They named the child Martin Luther King Jr.

2. The young Martin, growing amidst the gardens of his forebears, encountered the thorns of racial segregation. These early trials, though harsh and unjust, were to shape his heart and mind, forging within him a deep thirst for righteousness and equity among all of God's children.

3. In his quest for knowledge, Martin journeyed to the halls of Morehouse College, a bastion of learning where the young minds of his generation were kindled with the flames of wisdom and understanding.

4. With a spirit undeterred, he furthered his pilgrimage to Crozer Theological Seminary. There, amidst the seekers of divine truth, he delved into the sacred texts and teachings, seeking to unravel the mysteries of faith and its profound call to social justice.

5. The path of enlightenment led Martin to the venerable institution of Boston University. In this place of scholarly pursuit, he was bestowed with a doctorate, a symbol of his dedication to the pursuit of knowledge

and a testament to his preparedness for the greater task that awaited him.

Chapter 2: Rise as a Civil Rights Leader

1. And it came to pass in the year of our Lord, nineteen hundred and sixty-three that a great wind of change began to stir in Montgomery, a city in the land of Alabama. In this time and place, Martin Luther King Jr. rose as a beacon of hope, a leader among those who yearned for the waters of justice in a dry and parched land.

2. In those days, Black people were oppressed, forced to abide by the laws of segregation; laws that divided brother from brother, as the chaff is separated from the wheat. And in the midst of this affliction, the people cried out for a deliverer.

3. Martin, seeing the suffering of his brethren, stepped forth like David against Goliath, armed not with sword and shield, but with the power of nonviolence and words of truth. Inspired by the teachings of the prophet Gandhi and the Lord Jesus, he preached a gospel of peace and civil disobedience.

4. With eloquence and grace, he led the Montgomery Bus Boycott, a crusade against the chariots of segregation. For three hundred and eighty-one days, the people of Montgomery walked in unity, their feet treading the path of righteousness.

5. In the year of our Lord, nineteen hundred and fifty-seven, Martin, along with other shepherds of the people, founded the Southern Christian Leadership Conference. This fellowship of leaders sought to guide their flocks through the wilderness of discrimination and to the Promised Land of equality and justice.

6. Under his leadership, the Conference became a trumpet of justice, sounding forth a call to dismantle the walls of segregation and to let freedom ring throughout the land.

7. Martin's voice, a clarion call in the wilderness of inequality, echoed across

the hills and valleys of America, stirring the hearts of all who heard it. He spoke of a dream, a vision where all God's children, regardless of the color of their skin, would join hands in brotherhood and fellowship.

8. Thus, Martin Luther King Jr. ascended as a towering figure in the struggle for civil rights, a guiding star in the long night of oppression, leading his people towards the dawn of a new day of freedom and equality.

Chapter 3: Landmark Speeches and Writings

1. And it came to pass, in the year of our Lord nineteen hundred and sixty-three, that Martin Luther King Jr., a shepherd of his people, stood upon the steps of the Lincoln Memorial in the great assembly of the March on Washington.
2. With the multitudes gathered as a sea before him, he lifted his voice like a trumpet, and there flowed from his lips the dream of his heart, a vision of

Chapter 4: Significant Campaigns and Marches

1. And in those days, Martin Luther King Jr., a prophet of peace, led his people in a great journey from Selma unto Montgomery, a pilgrimage for the sacred right of voting, a right denied to many because of the color of their skin.
2. This march was like unto the crossing of the Red Sea, a passage from the bondage of disenfranchisement to the freedom of civic participation, a testament to the enduring spirit of those who thirsted for righteousness in the land.
3. King, with the staff of nonviolence in his hand, called forth a multitude of peaceful warriors. They assembled in streets and cities, a mighty river of

souls, flowing with the resolve to confront the Goliaths of racial injustice.

4. Their steps, though weary, resounded with the strength of hope; their voices, though often silenced, echoed with the hymns of freedom. Across the land, from the valleys of despair to the mountaintops of glory, they marched, a living testament to the power of unified hearts.

5. Yet, as they journeyed forth, they faced the fierce winds of resistance and the storms of hostility. Pharaohs of prejudice and rulers of discrimination sought to quell their righteous cause with the chariots of oppression and the horses of fear.

6. But Martin, a modern-day Moses, stood undaunted. His faith was as a shield, his words as a sword of truth. Amidst trials and tribulations, he held aloft the banner of nonviolence, a light that pierced the darkness, guiding his people through the wilderness of hatred and segregation.

7. Thus, through these campaigns and marches, King and his followers sowed the seeds of change in the hardened soil of inequality. They watered these seeds with the tears of their struggles and the blood of their sacrifices, nurturing the blossoming tree of freedom that would one day bear the fruits of justice for all.

Chapter 5: Nobel Peace Prize and Global Influence

1. In the year of our Lord nineteen hundred and sixty-four, a great honor was bestowed upon Martin, servant of peace and shepherd of equality. For his unyielding crusade against the Goliath of racial inequality and his steadfast adherence to the path of nonviolence, he was awarded the Nobel Peace Prize, a laurel of high esteem among the nations.

2. Behold, the name of Martin Luther King Jr. became as a shining star in the firmament of the world's peacemakers. Kings and commoners, elders and youths, from far-flung nations and diverse peoples, looked upon his works and marveled.

3. His teachings on nonviolent resistance, like precious seeds carried by the winds, found fertile ground in distant lands. In places torn by strife and

burdened by oppression, his words took root, sprouting into movements for freedom and justice.

4. As Moses before Pharaoh, so stood Martin before the powers of his time, proclaiming liberty to the captives and the opening of the prison to those who are bound. His philosophy of peaceful protest became a beacon of hope, a guiding light for those navigating the turbulent seas of social and political struggles.

5. Thus, the influence of Martin, a drum major for justice, resounded beyond the shores of his homeland.

Chapter 6: Challenges and Controversies

1. And as Martin Luther King Jr. journeyed forth on his divine mission, he was beset by trials and tribulations, for the path of righteousness is often strewn with thorns and stones.

2. He faced the Pharaohs of his time, rulers and authorities who sought to silence his voice and quench the spirit of freedom he kindled in the hearts of many.

3. Within the walls of his own community, there arose voices of dissent, brethren who questioned his methods and the slow unfolding of the promised victory. His heart was oftentimes grieved, for he sought unity in the struggle for liberation.

4. The scribes of the press and the scholars of the law scrutinized his every word and deed, seeking to find fault and sow seeds of doubt among the people he led.

5. In the courts of the land, he was accused and maligned, portrayed as a disturber of peace and order. Yet, in truth, he was a bearer of a higher peace, a divine order rooted in justice and equality.

6. In the midst of these fiery trials, Martin's faith was tested like gold in the furnace. He wrestled with the principalities and powers of darkness, yet his resolve remained unshaken, his vision unclouded.

7. For he knew that the arc of the moral universe, though long, bends

towards justice, and that truth crushed to earth will rise again.

8. Thus, in the face of challenges and controversies, Martin stood as a steadfast oak, rooted in the soil of truth and righteousness. His life, a living epistle, written not with ink but with the spirit of the living God, became a testament to the enduring power of love and nonviolence.

9. And though his journey on earth was marked by valleys of shadows, he feared no evil, for the Lord was with him, his rod and his staff, they comforted him. His legacy, a beacon of hope, continues to light the path for generations to come, guiding them towards the promised land of freedom and equality.

10.

VIII

Cultural Expressions

32

Music, Art, and Literature in Nocturnal Judaism

Nocturnal Judaism, deeply rooted in both Jewish and African heritage, expresses its rich cultural tapestry through various forms of art, including music, visual arts, and literature.

1. Music as a Spiritual and Cultural Vehicle:
   - Music plays a pivotal role in Nocturnal Judaism, blending traditional Jewish melodies with African and African-American rhythms and styles. These musical expressions are used not just in worship, but also as a means of storytelling, celebration, and spiritual connection.
   - Drumming, often used in African traditions to communicate and celebrate, is incorporated into religious ceremonies, providing a rhythmic backdrop to prayers and chants.

2. Visual Arts as a Reflection of Heritage:
   - Art in Nocturnal Judaism is a vibrant amalgamation of Jewish symbols and African motifs. This includes textiles, paintings, and sculptures that often depict biblical stories, spiritual concepts, and historical narratives from an Afrocentric perspective.

- Traditional Jewish art forms like calligraphy are reinterpreted, sometimes incorporating cuneiform script elements to acknowledge the ancient Near Eastern connections.

3. Literature Bridging Cultures and Traditions:
   - The literary contributions of Nocturnal Judaism include theological works, poetry, and stories that weave together Jewish teachings and African wisdom.
   - This literature often explores themes of exile, freedom, identity, and spirituality, reflecting the community's unique experiences and perspectives.

Influences of African and African-American Cultures

The rich cultural heritage of Africa and the African-American experience deeply influences the cultural expressions of Nocturnal Judaism.

1. African Influences:
   - Elements of African culture, including folklore, traditional practices, and spiritual beliefs, are interwoven into the fabric of Nocturnal Judaism, providing depth and a broad spectrum of expression.
   - African languages, motifs, and spiritual practices enrich the community's religious life and artistic expressions.

2. African-American Contributions:
   - The history and culture of African-Americans, particularly their experiences of struggle, resilience, and creativity, significantly shape the community's cultural identity.
   - The legacy of African-American music, from spirituals to jazz and blues, infuses the musical expressions of Nocturnal Judaism with a unique soulful and rhythmic quality.

Contemporary Expressions and Innovations

Nocturnal Judaism is dynamic, continually evolving to include contemporary expressions and innovations.

1. Modern Artistic Endeavors:
   - Artists within the community are creating new forms of expression that reflect current experiences and challenges, blending traditional elements with modern styles and mediums.
   - This includes digital art, multimedia installations, and modern interpretations of ancient musical styles.

2. Literary and Theological Evolution:
   - Contemporary writers and theologians in the community are exploring current issues through the lenses of Nocturnal Judaism, contributing to the ongoing dialogue between ancient teachings and modern realities.
   - These contributions keep the community's traditions vibrant and relevant, ensuring their continuity and evolution.

Conclusion

Chapter 6 highlights the rich cultural expressions of Nocturnal Judaism, showcasing how music, art, and literature serve as conduits for spiritual expression and cultural continuity. The integration of African and African-American influences with Jewish traditions creates a unique and dynamic cultural identity, continuously enriched by contemporary innovations and contributions.

33

Cultural Expressions

Music, Art, and Literature in Nocturnal Judaism

Nocturnal Judaism, deeply rooted in both Jewish and African heritage, expresses its rich cultural tapestry through various forms of art, including music, visual arts, and literature.

1. Music as a Spiritual and Cultural Vehicle:
   - Music plays a pivotal role in Nocturnal Judaism, blending traditional Jewish melodies with African and African-American rhythms and styles. These musical expressions are used not just in worship, but also as a means of storytelling, celebration, and spiritual connection.
   - Drumming, often used in African traditions to communicate and celebrate, is incorporated into religious ceremonies, providing a rhythmic backdrop to prayers and chants.

2. Visual Arts as a Reflection of Heritage:
   - Art in Nocturnal Judaism is a vibrant amalgamation of Jewish symbols and African motifs. This includes textiles, paintings, and sculptures that often depict biblical stories, spiritual concepts, and historical narratives from an Afrocentric perspective.
   - Traditional Jewish art forms like calligraphy are reinterpreted, sometimes

incorporating cuneiform script elements to acknowledge the ancient Near Eastern connections.

3. Literature Bridging Cultures and Traditions:
   - The literary contributions of Nocturnal Judaism include theological works, poetry, and stories that weave together Jewish teachings and African wisdom.
   - This literature often explores themes of exile, freedom, identity, and spirituality, reflecting the community's unique experiences and perspectives.

Influences of African and African-American Cultures

The rich cultural heritage of Africa and the African-American experience deeply influences the cultural expressions of Nocturnal Judaism.

1. African Influences:
   - Elements of African culture, including folklore, traditional practices, and spiritual beliefs, are interwoven into the fabric of Nocturnal Judaism, providing depth and a broad spectrum of expression.
   - African languages, motifs, and spiritual practices enrich the community's religious life and artistic expressions.

2. African-American Contributions:
   - The history and culture of African-Americans, particularly their experiences of struggle, resilience, and creativity, significantly shape the community's cultural identity.
   - The legacy of African-American music, from spirituals to jazz and blues, infuses the musical expressions of Nocturnal Judaism with a unique soulful and rhythmic quality.

Contemporary Expressions and Innovations

Nocturnal Judaism is dynamic, continually evolving to include contemporary expressions and innovations.

1. Modern Artistic Endeavors:

  - Artists within the community are creating new forms of expression that reflect current experiences and challenges, blending traditional elements with modern styles and mediums.

  - This includes digital art, multimedia installations, and modern interpretations of ancient musical styles.

2. Literary and Theological Evolution:

  - Contemporary writers and theologians in the community are exploring current issues through the lenses of Nocturnal Judaism, contributing to the ongoing dialogue between ancient teachings and modern realities.

  - These contributions keep the community's traditions vibrant and relevant, ensuring their continuity and evolution.

This chapter highlights the rich cultural expressions of Nocturnal Judaism, showcasing how music, art, and literature serve as conduits for spiritual expression and cultural continuity. The integration of African and African-American influences with Jewish traditions creates a unique and dynamic cultural identity, continuously enriched by contemporary innovations and contributions.

34

Community and Identity

In Nocturnal Judaism, the community plays a central role in shaping individual identities, fostering spiritual growth, and preparing members for the challenges of the real world.

1. Supportive Environment for Growth:
   - The community provides a nurturing environment where members can explore their spirituality, culture, and individual talents. It's a space where personal ideas and life plans are encouraged and supported, emphasizing their potential to contribute positively to the world.
   - Educational programs, mentor

2. Fostering a Sense of Belonging and Purpose:
   - The community acts as a nurturing space where individuals can explore their identity, beliefs, and purpose. Through shared experiences, rituals, and teachings, members develop a strong sense of belonging and an understanding of their role within both the Jewish and African-American narratives.

2. Educational and Spiritual Development:
   - Education is a cornerstone of community life in Nocturnal Judaism, encompassing both traditional Jewish learning and teachings from African

and African-American heritage. This holistic approach prepares individuals to navigate the complexities of the modern world while staying rooted in their cultural and spiritual identities.

- Spiritual guidance and mentorship are provided, helping members to integrate ethical teachings and spiritual practices into their daily lives.

Challenges and Opportunities for Identity Formation

The unique intersection of Jewish and African-American cultures in Nocturnal Judaism presents both challenges and opportunities for identity formation.

1. Navigating Dual Heritage:
- Members of the community often navigate a dual heritage, balancing their Jewish identity with their African-American roots. This can present challenges, especially in contexts where one aspect of their identity is not well understood or accepted.
- The community provides a supportive environment to explore and reconcile these dual aspects, enabling members to form a cohesive and empowered identity.

2. Embracing Diversity Within the Community:
- Nocturnal Judaism is marked by diversity, not just in terms of race and culture, but also in interpretations of religious and spiritual practices. This diversity is seen as a strength, offering a wealth of perspectives and experiences.

Engagement with Wider Jewish and Black Communities

Nocturnal Judaism actively engages with both the wider Jewish and Black communities, recognizing the importance of these interactions in shaping its identity and impact.

1. Dialogue and Collaboration:

- There is an emphasis on dialogue and collaboration with other Jewish communities, fostering mutual understanding and respect. This engagement allows for the sharing of traditions and teachings, enriching the Jewish experience for all involved.

- Similarly, connections with broader African-American communities are nurtured, often focusing on shared experiences and struggles. This fosters solidarity and joint initiatives, especially in areas of social justice and community development.

2. Addressing Misconceptions and Building Bridges:

- The community often faces the task of addressing misconceptions about their dual identity. Education and open dialogue play crucial roles in breaking down stereotypes and fostering understanding.

- By participating in interfaith and intercultural dialogues

In Nocturnal Judaism, the community serves as both a sanctuary and a forge, shaping individuals' identities and preparing them for the broader challenges of the world.

1. Nurturing Individual Potential:

- The community places a high emphasis on discovering and nurturing the unique talents and abilities of each member. Education and spiritual guidance are tailored to help individuals realize their potential and align their personal aspirations with a greater purpose.

2. Creating a Supportive Environment:

- Members are encouraged to support one another's endeavors, creating an environment where ideas can flourish. This support extends beyond spiritual and emotional assistance to include practical help in pursuing

35

The Nocturnal Jewish Perspective on Tithes

Beyond Monetary Offerings: Tithing Time, Talents, and Resources

In the unique practice of Nocturnal Judaism, the concept of tithes extends far beyond the traditional monetary contributions commonly associated with many religious traditions. This chapter delves into the rich and multifaceted understanding of tithing within the Nocturnal Jewish community, highlighting its emphasis on community support, personal growth, and communal responsibility.

1. Redefining Tithes: A Holistic Approach

At the heart of Nocturnal Judaism's approach to tithes is the belief that contributing to the community involves more than just financial support. Members are encouraged to give 10% of their gifts, talents, and time. This holistic approach recognizes that every individual has unique contributions to make, whether it be in the form of creative skills, professional expertise, or personal time.

2. Tithing from the Garden and Business Ventures

For those engaged in agriculture or business, the traditional concept of tithing takes on a tangible form. Members who cultivate gardens are encouraged to contribute 10% of their crops, an act that not only supports communal needs but also reinforces a connection to the land and nature. Business owners, similarly, are urged to allocate 10% of their business resources or profits, fostering a culture of generosity and mutual support within the community.

3. Volunteering Time: Strengthening Community Bonds

Recognizing the value of personal involvement, Nocturnal Jews are encouraged to dedicate 10% of their time to community service. This could include various activities like mentoring, assisting in communal projects, or participating in the maintenance of communal spaces. Such engagement not only strengthens the community but also enriches the individual's sense of belonging and purpose.

4. Mentorship and Training: Investing in the Future

A pivotal aspect of the Nocturnal Jewish approach to tithes is the focus on mentorship and training, particularly for the youth. By offering guidance in areas ranging from arts to practical skills, community members invest in the younger generation, helping keep them engaged and out of trouble. This investment in youth is seen not just as a contribution but as a sacred duty to pass on knowledge and values.

5. Recycling and Sharing Resources

In a testament to the community's commitment to sustainability and support, members are encouraged to donate items like furniture, which are then refurbished and redistributed to those in need. This practice not only recycles valuable resources but also ensures that every community member's basic needs are met, reinforcing the principle of collective welfare.

6. The Impact of Non-Monetary Tithing

This broader interpretation of tithing creates a dynamic and interconnected community where each member feels valued and essential.

After conducting a thorough search in the provided documents, I did not find specific information on Nocturnal Judaism's beliefs about tithes. The concept of tithing, as you described, where members contribute not just monetarily but also through their gifts, talents, time, and other resources like crops and business contributions, is not explicitly detailed in the available materials.

This unique approach to tithing, emphasizing community support and personal growth through various forms of contributions, reflects a holistic and communal ethos. It aligns with the broader themes of mentorship, training, and resource sharing for the welfare of the community, especially for the youth. However, for more detailed insights or specific doctrines on this topic within Nocturnal Judaism, additional or more specific sources would be needed.

IX

Modern Challeges

36

Modern Challenges and Future Directions

Nocturnal Judaism, while deeply rooted in ancient traditions, faces the continuous challenge of navigating the modern world. Balancing tradition with modernity is a key focus for the community.

1. Adapting Ancient Wisdom to Contemporary Life:
   - The community actively works to find relevance in ancient teachings for contemporary issues, ensuring that traditional wisdom guides modern living. This involves interpreting traditional scriptures and practices in ways that speak to the current experiences of the community.

2. Technology and Tradition:
   - In an era dominated by technology, Nocturnal Judaism explores ways to utilize these tools without losing the essence of traditional practices. Whether it's through online study groups or virtual celebrations of festivals, the community seeks a balance that honors tradition while embracing modern advancements.

Interfaith and Intercultural Relations

As a community with a unique blend of Jewish and African-American heritage, Nocturnal Judaism places great importance on interfaith and intercultural relations.

1. Dialogue and Collaboration:
   - The community actively engages in dialogue with other Jewish and Black communities, as well as with groups from different religious and cultural backgrounds. This dialogue aims to foster mutual understanding, respect, and collaboration.

2. Educational Outreach:
   - Educational programs are designed not just for internal community-building but also to educate others about the unique aspects of Nocturnal Judaism. This outreach helps demystify the practices of the community and build bridges with broader society.

Vision for the Future of Nocturnal Judaism

Looking forward, Nocturnal Judaism is focused on shaping a vision that ensures its sustainability and relevance for future generations.

1. Youth Engagement:
   - Recognizing that youth are the future, there is a strong emphasis on engaging younger members of the community. This includes education tailored to be relevant and appealing to younger audiences, as well as involving them in leadership and decision-making processes.

2. Sustainability and Growth:

- The community is working on strategies to sustain and grow its membership and resources. This includes developing financial strategies, community services, and programs that address the needs of all members.

3. Global Perspective:
- With the increasing globalization of societies, Nocturnal Judaism seeks to develop a global perspective. This involves understanding and addressing issues that affect people worldwide, and recognizing that the community is part of a larger, interconnected world.

Nocturnal Judaism explores the challenges and opportunities the community faces in the modern world. Balancing tradition with modernity, engaging in interfaith and intercultural dialogues, and crafting a vision for the future are pivotal aspects of the community's journey. By addressing these challenges head-on and with a clear direction, Nocturnal Judaism aims to remain a vibrant and relevant force in the lives of its members and the wider community.

37

Introduction to Nocturnal Judaism 101

As we bring to a close the enlightening saga of "Nocturnal Judaism: A Beacon in the Night," we stand on the cusp of a deeper foray into this distinctive and spirited faith tradition. Our odyssey thus far has been revelatory, unearthing the intricate mosaic of Nocturnal Judaism — its historical roots, spiritual practices, cultural manifestations, and its profound influence on its adherents, especially within the African-American community.

Yet, our exploration is far from over. The allure of Nocturnal Judaism, with its rich amalgamation of traditions, beliefs, and rituals, calls us to delve into one of its most enchanting and celebratory facets — its feast festivals and holidays. Here, the pulse of the community is most palpable, where the melding of African heritage and Jewish customs vibrates in a celebration of life, introspection, and solidarity.

As we eagerly await the next volume, we extend an invitation to immerse yourself in the jubilant celebrations of Nocturnal Judaism's festivals and holidays. The upcoming book promises a vivid odyssey across the lunar calendar, examining the historical foundations, spiritual essence, and the distinctive observances of these hallowed times in Nocturnal Judaism. From the introspective solemnity of Yom Kippur to the exultant emancipation of Passover, each festival weaves its own unique story into the splendid tapestry of Nocturnal Jewish life.

Envision immersing in the vibrant tales of these celebrations, where time-honored Jewish traditions seamlessly intertwine with the rhythms and rituals of African heritage. Visualize the community uniting not only in pious prayer but in exuberant dance, song, and communal feasting, each festival a moment to reaffirm their faith, heritage, and communal bonds.

This book, however, aims to be more than a mere chronicle of festivities. It aspires to be a conduit to the profound significance behind these celebrations, shedding light on how they enrich understanding of identity and purpose. It also seeks to illustrate how these festivals act as a bridge, linking the Nocturnal Jewish community with the broader Jewish and African-American communities, enhancing mutual understanding and appreciation of this unique cultural and spiritual journey.

Prepare to be enthralled by tales of endurance and freedom, stirred by the cadences of ancient songs, and enlightened by the deep wisdom embedded in each festival and holiday. The forthcoming book is set to be a thrilling continuation of our journey into Nocturnal Judaism, showcasing its elegance, resilience, and dynamism.

As we eagerly await this new chapter, let's continue to nurture the spirit of discovery, understanding, and community we've cultivated through "Nocturnal Judaism: Modern Perspectives." The adventure moves forward, promising even more enriching insights. Stay tuned for a captivating exploration of Nocturnal Judaism's feast festivals and holidays, a celebration where history, culture, and spirituality intertwine beneath the moon's radiant gaze.

X

Appendices

<h1 style="text-align:center">38</h1>

Summary of Key Points from "Nocturnal Judaism: Modern Perspectives

Introduction to Nocturnal Judaism

- Overview of unique aspects of Nocturnal Judaism, emphasizing its blend of traditional Jewish teachings and African-American cultural perspectives.
    - Discussion of methodology and sources used in the formation of Nocturnal Judaism, respecting and aligning with its distinctive historical context.

Core Beliefs and Principles

- Exploration of basic tenets unique to Nocturnal Judaism, including its approach to integrating African spiritual heritage.
    - Emphasis on lunar wisdom, the significance of nighttime practices, and the community's focus on self-reliance in manufacturing and distribution.

Sacred Texts and Literature

- Examination of key texts, including the Hebrew Bible, Cuneiform writings, and the Tashlultum Mishna.
    - Unique interpretative methods combining traditional Jewish hermeneutics with African-American cultural heritage.
    - Contributions of Black scholars and leaders in shaping the community's understanding and approach to these sacred texts.

Rituals and Practices

- Daily practices specific to Nocturnal Judaism, emphasizing evening study, nocturnal prayers, and dream interpretation.
    - Observances of Sabbath and holidays, integrating traditional Jewish rituals with African and African-American cultural expressions.
    - Description of rites of passage and community celebrations, blending Jewish traditions with African heritage.

The Three Pilgrimages and Daily Purpose

- Description of the metaphorical pilgrimages of Sugarplum, Daydream, and Nightmare, each representing different life stages.
    - Alignment of daily activities with the seven days of creation, infusing each day with specific spiritual and practical significance.

Cultural Expressions

- The role of music, art, and literature in Nocturnal Judaism as mediums for spiritual expression and cultural continuity.
    - Influence of African and African-American cultures in shaping the community's artistic expressions.
    - Discussion on contemporary expressions and innovations within the community, highlighting modern artistic and literary contributions.

Community and Identity

- The importance of the community in nurturing individual potential and creating a supportive environment.
   - Discussion of the challenges and opportunities in identity formation, particularly in navigating modernity and maintaining traditions.
   - Engagement with the wider Jewish and Black communities to foster understanding and collaboration.

Modern Challenges and Future Directions

- Navigating the balance between tradition and modernity, including the use of technology.
   - Importance of interfaith and intercultural relations for community growth and understanding.
   - Vision for the future of Nocturnal Judaism, focusing on youth engagement, sustainability, and adopting a global perspective.

Throughout the book, "Nocturnal Judaism: Modern Perspectives," there is a consistent emphasis on the integration of Jewish traditions with African-American history and culture, reflecting a unique spiritual path. The community's approach to sacred texts, rituals, cultural expressions, and modern challenges highlights its adaptability and commitment to maintaining a vibrant and relevant identity.

39

Glossary of Terms from "Nocturnal Judaism: Modern Perspectives

1. Nocturnal Judaism: A unique form of Judaism that combines traditional Jewish teachings with African-American cultural and spiritual practices, with a particular emphasis on nighttime rituals and lunar cycles.

2. Tashlultum Mishna: A collection of writings significant to Nocturnal Judaism, offering interpretations of Jewish law and philosophy through an African-American lens.

3. Sugarplum: One of the three metaphorical pilgrimages in Nocturnal Judaism, symbolizing joy, contentment, and the sweetness of life.

4. Daydream: Another pilgrimage in Nocturnal Judaism, representing aspiration, hope, and the pursuit of a better future.

5. Nightmare: The third pilgrimage, symbolizing challenges and struggles in life, and teaching resilience and strength.

6. Sozo Keys: Concept in Nocturnal Judaism referring to specific vibrational energies of sounds or musical notes, used in sound healing and spiritual practices.

7. Torah Portion: A section of the Torah read weekly in Jewish tradition. In Nocturnal Judaism, a person's birth date Torah portion is significant for personal and spiritual development.

8. Bo: A specific Torah portion (Exodus 10:1), representing themes of liberation and leadership, used for spiritual reflection in Nocturnal Judaism.

9. Sh'vat: A month in the Jewish lunar calendar, used in Nocturnal Judaism for aligning spiritual practices with specific Torah portions.

10. Akkadian Cuneiform: Ancient script and texts from the Akkadian Empire, integrated into Nocturnal Judaism's study and spiritual practices.

11. Lunar Cycle: The phases of the moon, which are of significant spiritual and ritual importance in Nocturnal Judaism.

12. African Spiritual Heritage: Elements of traditional African spirituality incorporated into Nocturnal Judaism.

13. Spiritual and Ethical Teachings: Core principles and teachings in Nocturnal Judaism that guide moral conduct and spiritual growth.

14. Interfaith and Intercultural Relations: The practice of engaging in dialogue and collaboration with different religious and cultural groups, significant in Nocturnal Judaism for community building and understanding.

15. Cultural Expressions: Forms of artistic and creative expression in Nocturnal Judaism, including music, art, and literature, that reflect its unique blend of Jewish and African-American heritage.

By understanding these terms, readers can gain deeper insight into the unique practices and beliefs of Nocturnal Judaism and its place in the contemporary religious landscape.

40

Meaning of "Night"

Dictionary Description for "Night"

Night (noun):

1. Literal Definition:
   - The period of darkness between sunset and sunrise when the sky is devoid of sunlight. It is characterized by increased activity for nocturnal creatures and is governed by the moon and stars in their celestial movements.

2. Metaphorical Definitions:
   - Soul Realm: In various philosophical and spiritual contexts, 'night' metaphorically represents the soul realm. This is a conceptual space for introspection, where the deeper aspects of one's inner life and spirituality are explored. It's a time for the soul to engage in self-reflection, away from the distractions of the external world.
   - Nocturnal Realm: Symbolically, 'night' can refer to the nocturnal realm, a domain where activities and energies that thrive under the cover of darkness come to life. Governed by the moon, this metaphorical realm often symbolizes mystery, the subconscious, and aspects of life that are hidden or underexplored.
   - Jewish Metaphors for Night:

- Time for Study and Prayer: In Jewish tradition, night is often seen as an ideal time for Torah study and prayer, offering quiet and solitude conducive to spiritual deepening.

- Exile and Redemption: In some interpretations, 'night' represents periods of exile or spiritual darkness, with the hopeful anticipation of a 'dawn' of redemption and enlightenment.

- Cycle of Renewal: Night also symbolizes the end of a day, leading to renewal and a new beginning, reflecting the constant cycle of life and spiritual rejuvenation.

- Other Cultural Metaphors:

- Rest and Restoration: Commonly across cultures, night is associated with rest and the restoration of energy, symbolizing a time of peace and rejuvenation.

- Unknown and Unconscious: Night often represents the unknown or unconscious parts of the human psyche, mirroring the hidden or obscure aspects of life and the universe.

In literature and philosophy, 'night' is a versatile term rich with symbolic meaning. Its representation ranges from the literal absence of daylight to various metaphorical concepts, each providing a unique lens through which different aspects of the human experience are understood and interpreted.